A.C.H.I.E.V.E

ROBBIE MOTTER

HAVANABOOKGROUPLLC
HAVANABOOKGROUP.COM

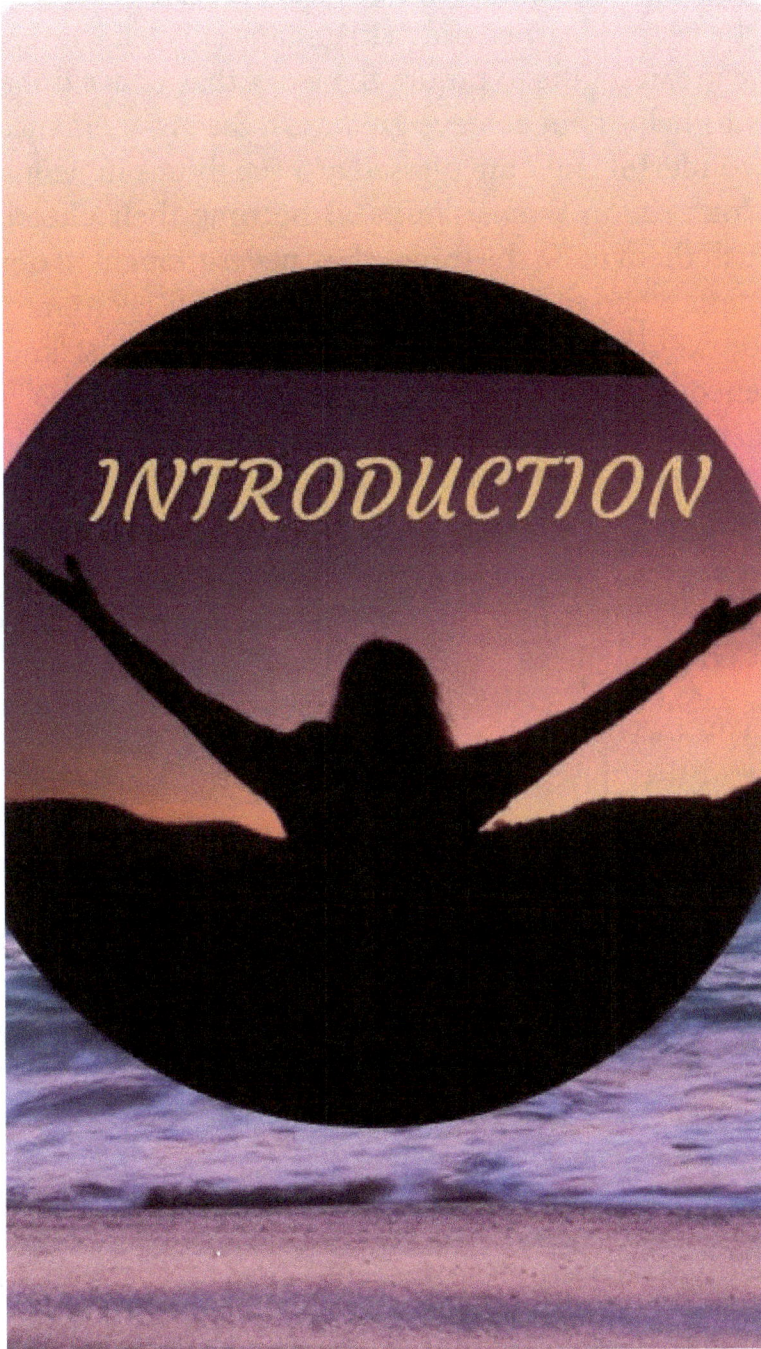

INTRODUCTION

My name is Robbie Motter, I am 86 years old. I have had an amazing career in Corporate America and as an entrepreneur. Over the years, I learned much to enhance my leadership skills but the greatest gifts to me are the work that I have done with others to help them achieve greatness. Seeing their successes is so wonderful and I am blessed as I see things in people that they don't see in themselves, so I become their cheerleader and push them to do the things they never thought of doing. It never fails when they achieve them, they will say to me "How did you know I could do that?" and I say, "I just knew." I have encouraged women to do radio shows, write their book not just talk about it, to learn to speak as everyone has a story to share, to step out and take steps out of their comfort zone, dream big, and most of all to be real with high integrity and to step out and help others. When I meet new people, I immediately think who do I need to introduce this person to and I take immediate action.

Have you in your career run into women that you asked for help, and they just were too busy or just did not care? How about women that gossiped and were a little nasty to you on your way up the corporate ladder?

Well in 1970 that happened to me, I asked a co-worker in Nebraska to show me how to do something and she said, "I am too busy", and I don't have time to help women!" Wow, that shocked me away as in my life I learned at an early age that it was not about me but what I could do to help others and to make a difference.

As I talked to other women on the way up the corporate ladder, I heard the same stories. So in 70"s I made a pact with myself that I would step out and help women soar to greatness by mentoring and educating them, introducing them to people they needed to meet. I shared opportunities with them, showing them how to collaborate with others and teaching them that by also helping others they too will reap rewards.

I have personally seen benefits to me for helping others like: Less Stress and Tension, I find that helping others brings joy to me, gives me so much emotional satisfaction and happiness to see them achieve, so every day I try to touch a life.

While working in New York in a top corporate position, I also became the volunteer global coordinator for National Association of Female Executives (NAFE) a volunteer position. I spent over 29 years, interacting with their members all over the US and when (NAFE) decided to go another direction I formed my Global Society for Female Entrepreneurs a 501 c3 nonprofit so that I could continue to serve women globally.

My last two corporate positions one in New York with over 100 reporting to me and the last one in Virginia where I had over 200 employees really helped to enhance my leadership skills. I made sure also that I was always there for the employees to help them grow and learn. Several years ago, one gentleman who worked for me in New York and one woman who worked for me in Virginia found me on Facebook and told me "That in their whole career I was the best manager and mentor they ever had, and it helped them achieve to greater heights in their careers and that they were most grateful". It was so nice to hear all that they had accomplished, and I was happy that I played a part in their success. I am still in touch with many of my former employees in all the different states and positions I worked at and it's great to hear how their careers have grown over the years.

In 2017 I formed my nonprofit Global Society for Female Entrepreneurs (GSFE), where I serve as a volunteer and founder/CEO, this 501(c)(3) nonprofit organization works hand and hand with our networks to provide a variety of monthly meetings. These meetings are both on zoom and live not only in the US but International as well. GSFE provides personal and professional growth to Members through monthly meetings, training, mentoring and annual conferences. GSFE is in collaboration with other groups that are also touching lives of women. One such group is She Inspires Me, founded and run by Ada Gartenmann from London, England. On April 2, 2022, She Inspires Me will come to Long Beach CA. SIMA LOVE GALA will be an event that recognizes and awards women for their unselfish acts of inspiring women to achieve greater heights. GSFE has the opportunity to be part of this and almost 100 of our deserving women will be receiving awards.

No one does what they do for awards but it's always nice to get recognized by our peers. I am most honored as since 1980 I have received over 160 awards from Presidents of the United States, Presidents of Companies, non-profits, and other organizations as well as from US Senators and Congressman and CA Assembly, CA Senators and Cities. I have had the opportunity to present deserving and outstanding members with these same awards.

I remember one woman I nominated for an award who does great things for women in Orange County, CA with her women's organization and who has done them for over ten years called me when she found out that I nominated her and that she was a winner.

This is what she said, "No one had ever nominated me for an award". Wow, she was most deserving. I am so thrilled I could do that for her, she is a really amazing person.

Women also need to know the power of SHOWING UP. To

me SHOWING UP is like a treasure map and one never knows what treasure they will find when they SHOW UP, but I can tell you there are many. As a matter of fact, I could probably write ten books on the stories I have heard from my members on all the great things that happened to them once they started SHOWING UP and ASKING.

ASKING is another great power tool, for years women were always helpers and would never ask. I have been on a mission since the 70's teaching women the POWER of ASKING and its profound. Most don't ASK because they think they are going to get a NO.

Before you ASK you need to really know what you need and why you need it, then take the risk and ASK. If someone says NO, you are no worse off than when you started.

I just learned two new words that I now use when I get a NO and that is WHY NOT! Remember if someone says yes, you are a lot better off. Did you ever think that just by asking you could get a job, a raise, discounts for numerous things, items donated for events you are doing, sponsors and the list goes on and on.

I am everyday woman just like you are striving every day to ACHIEVE.

I love the word ACHIEVE as it has so many possibilities for success.

I took the word and came up with a word for each letter that meant something to me, and it seems always to keep me on track. So here are my words:

Table Of Contents

ACTION

A in the word Achieve to me means ACTION.

We can have lots of ideas or goals but if we don't take action nothing happens.

We never really realize all the steps it takes to take action as we just do it and many times, we don't figure out all the steps and we end up forgetting stuff. Action is powerful and it should be thought out and that way the results can even be bigger than originally imagined!

The dictionary says, ACTION – "The fact or process of doing something typically to achieve an aim."

I do lots of events and each one requires action, so I am going to use what I do when planning an event.

First, I need to make a decision on the date of the event, the location and the time. Then I put a budget together which includes the income for things like tickets, estimate for basket raffle, silent auction, and any other raffles. Additionally, I estimate the sponsorship I would receive. On the expenses side, I list rental cost for the facility, food cost, printing for flyers, tickets, marketing pieces and any other documents.

If I am mailing out in-kind letters, I include envelopes and postage costs. I always build in a miscellaneous cost to cover audio and sound and other unforeseen ancillary items. That is the first Action step, when I see the figures, it gives me an idea as to how much I need for sponsorships. This step also gives me an idea of what to charge for the tickets to attend the event. Sponsorships range for my events from $250.00 to $2,000 so the action step on this would be to look at the range, figure out each range what the sponsor would get, then create the sponsor sheets.

The next action step for me would be to make a list of names who I feel might consider being a sponsor and then sending them the sponsor package. I also include sponsor logos on the marketing flyers for the event, taking early action is necessary as many sponsors allocate funds on a first come basis if the request aligns with their services.

The next action step I would take is creating the in-kind donation letters for items to go into the baskets, and then figuring out who will I be contacting to ask for donations, so early action is critical in putting together a successful event.

Next action step for me would be to do a save the date flyer as people get busy and I want to make sure they add our event on their schedule and I set a deadline for those attending to purchase their tickets, as selling them ahead of time gives the person doing the event an idea of how much food to order.

Another action step for me would be to figure out the decorative theme and color and centerpieces and start pulling all that together or the action step could be to sit with the catering individual at the location of the event and plan the menu and decorations needed for the event. To me that action step needs to be done early as you can add the menu and other things in your marketing flyer.

I think we really don't take time to really think of all the action steps we take on everything we do as its such an important step.

Take time and make a list one day of all the action steps you take to accomplish what you do; it could be as simple as going to your place of employment think of all the steps you have to take action on just to achieve that.

I did that one day on all the things I did that day, and it was over 100 action steps taken to accomplish what I had to do. Once you do that you will see how important the word ACTION is as part of Achieving.

I took action when I decided to write my book "It's All About Showing Up and the POWER is in the ASKING. This book was published Jan 2021 with 46 coauthors and made #1 Best seller in US first day, and #1 International Best seller the next day. It has been picked up by major bookstores all over the world.

I took action with my life, I was raised in 26 foster homes, and at 14 I left and got on a greyhound bus and knew I had to get a job to start my life. I looked older, dressed in a suit I interviewed with a company and was hired, that company was Levi Strauss. I continued to take action to learn all I could at that company and every company I worked at in my life, I kept advancing in my career. I held many top corporate positions across the country including in New York with large staffs until I decided to be an entrepreneur and serve women.

Remember your past has nothing to do with your future, you are in charge… As to me obstacles are opportunities waiting to happen.

What are you doing to take action?

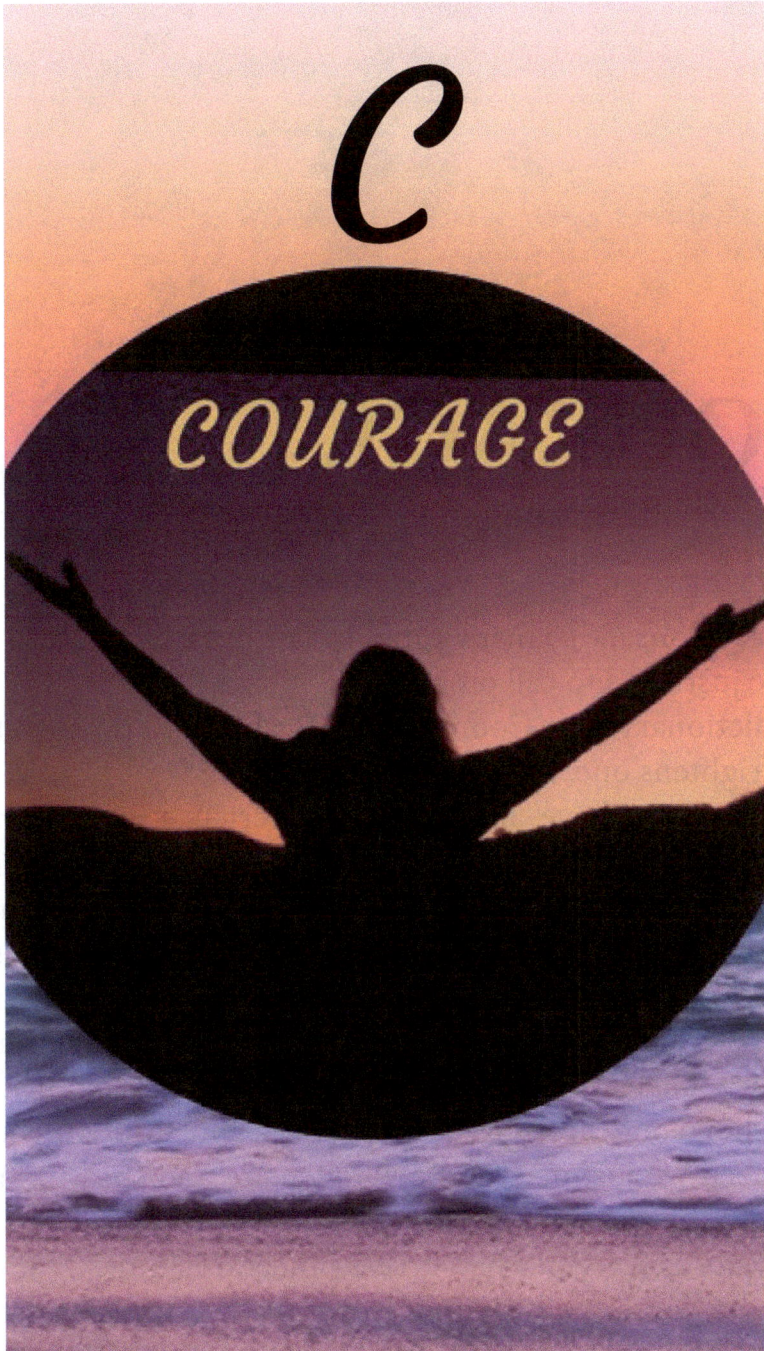

COURAGE

C is for Courage.

We need courage so many times in our lives, it's really in all of us, we just need to call on it.

The dictionary says Courage – "The ability to do something that frightens one.

I am sure we have all had that experience many times. I remember when I did "SUE TALK" it was tough as although I had spoken for years to crowds up to 10,000 people, I never had to memorize a talk, but for this one it was 12 minutes and it had to be memorized. I wanted to give up so many times. After the talk there was a break, and I had a lineup at my vendor table telling me how much my talk inspired them and how they could feel my passion and again through courage I realized we just need to be who we are and speak what we know to the audience can experience and feel it.

Ten years ago, when I had breast cancer, I had the courage to trust the doctor and to do what he said was necessary to get rid of the cancer and that was to remove my left breast and courage told me it would be okay and I would be healed, and

so far, I have been cancer free for ten years,
As a single mom with three children a son and two daughters I needed courage so many times, but it was always there for me. Courage is inside all of us we just need to pull it up. So, take time and think of events that you have had to have courage.
I shared with you some of my experiences, what have some of your experiences been in having courage. Living life fully takes courage!
Did you know that taking steps and having courage can build your self-esteem?
When you take steps to add courage in your life you strengthen that skill, share it, you will empower others to also add courage to their lives.

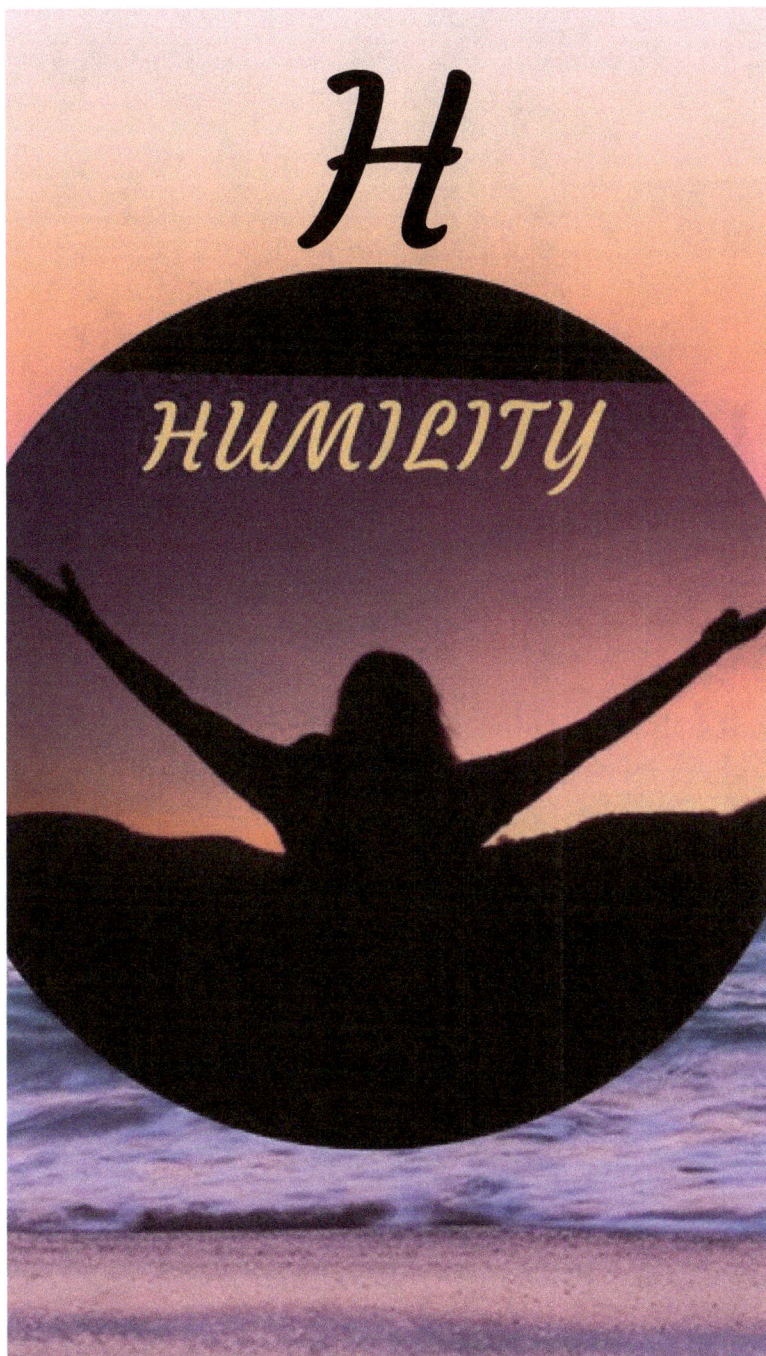

H

HUMILITY

HUMILTY

H is Humility

The quality of being humble. In the olden days they said just take care of you and forget everyone else, but that's not true today. It's about helping others as together we can do more and will achieve more. Remember, we are not in competition we are in collaboration.

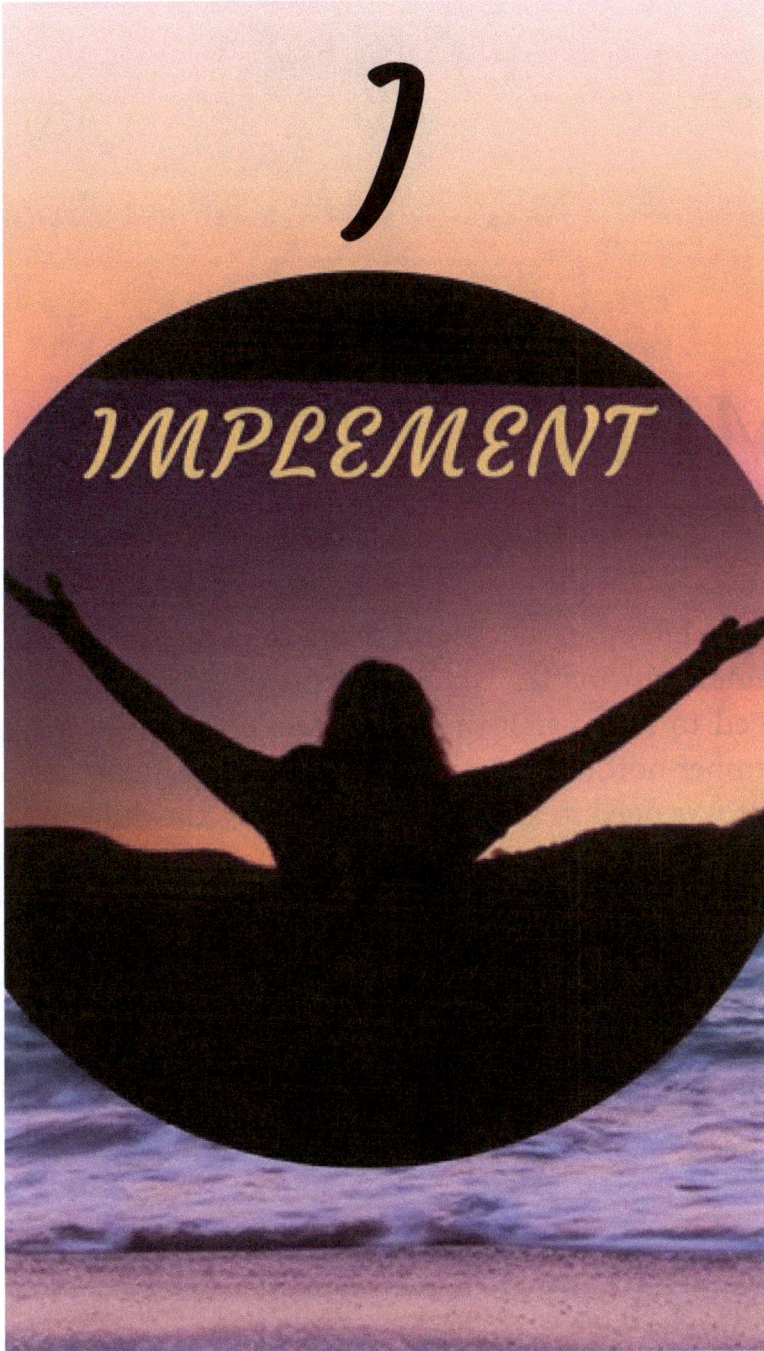

7

IMPLEMENT

IMPLEMENT

I is Implement.

Put into effect. A decision, plan, or agreement We must implement no matter what we want to do we need a plan; we need to look at all the steps it takes to make it happen. Remember nothing happens unless we implement our plan or project. We need to look at all that needs to be done. Example: Does it involve others? Is it on social media?

When I did my book, I had 46 coauthors. That meant one of the steps was to get them on board, get their stories, have them edited, and get the publisher in place. I got Havana Book Group, to edit, format, and design the cover. So, what steps do you need to take to implement your passions? How many years have you been saying you're going to write a book?

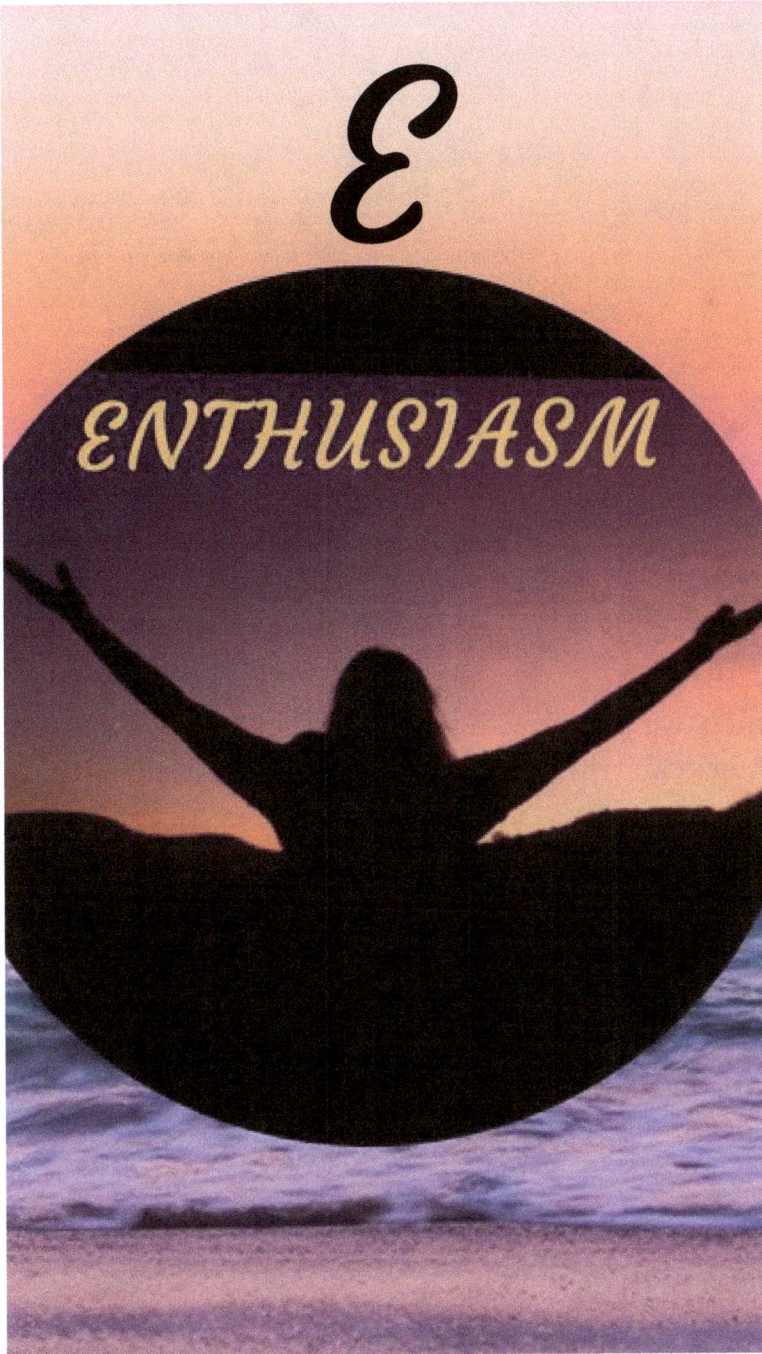

E

ENTHUSIASM

ENTHUSIASM
E is for Enthusiasm.

Intense and eager enjoyment, interest, or approval. I have found that when I am enthusiastic about a project it flows extremely well. In fact, in November of 2021 while I was at my daughter's cabin in Lake Arrowhead, I was so enthusiastic about Nominating women for the "She Inspires Me" Award. This is a prestigious award for women done by Ada Gartenmann of SIMA (She Inspires Me) in England for women all over the world. I wrote 80 nominations for 80 dynamic and deserving members and sent them to England for review. These awards will be presented at a Gala Entertainment dinner event Apr 2, 2022, in Long Beach, CA, which is exciting. So, what are you Enthusiastic about?

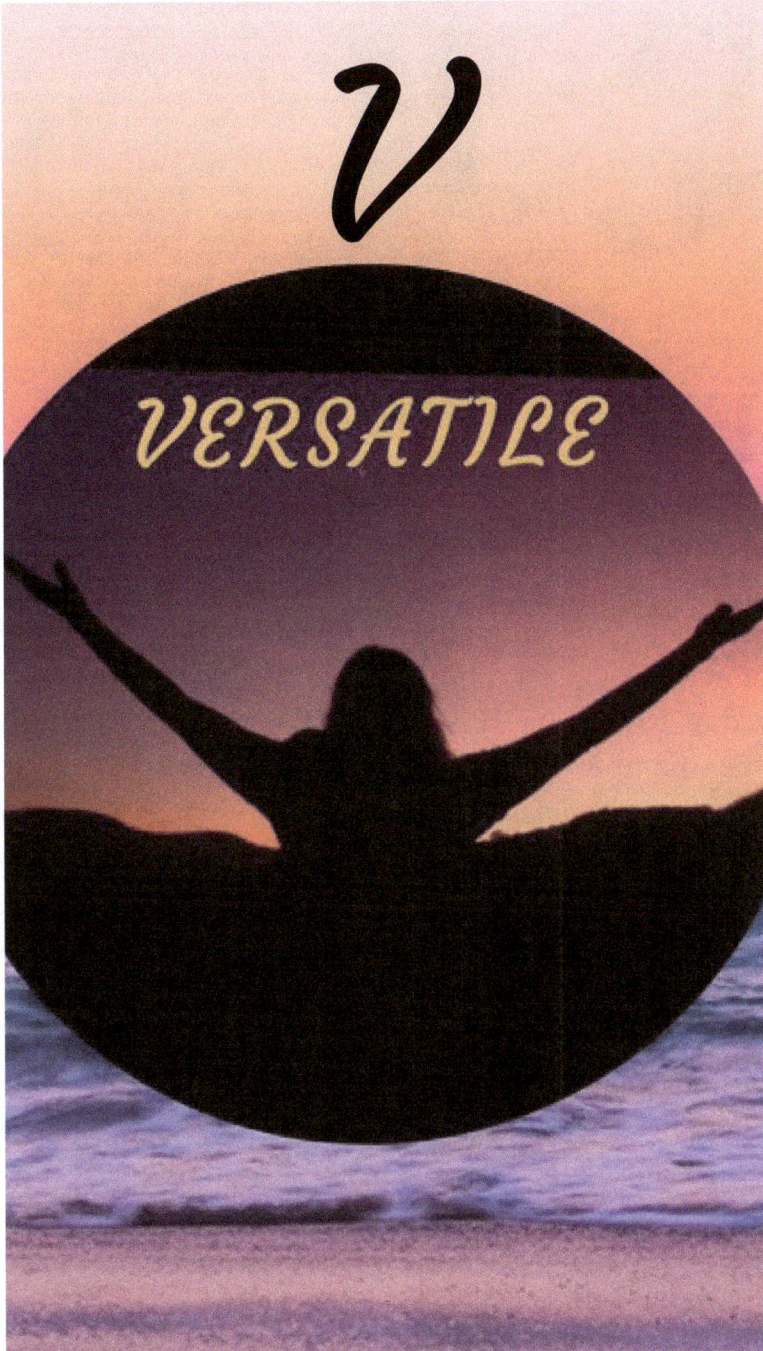

VERSATILE

V is Versatile.

Able to adopt or being able to do many different functions and/or activities.

Every day I must be versatile as I have over 350 members and the memberships are continually growing. My GSFE nonprofit has chapters from all over California. Nationally we are expanding in other States and Internationally, therefore I need to be there for them. So sometimes it means for me that the plans I have need to be changed, so that I can take care of the matters at hand. Many times, people don't do anything they keep waiting for perfect. There is no perfect time! Just step out, step up and do it, changes can be made along the way. So be flexible, think out of the box and be versatile where needed.

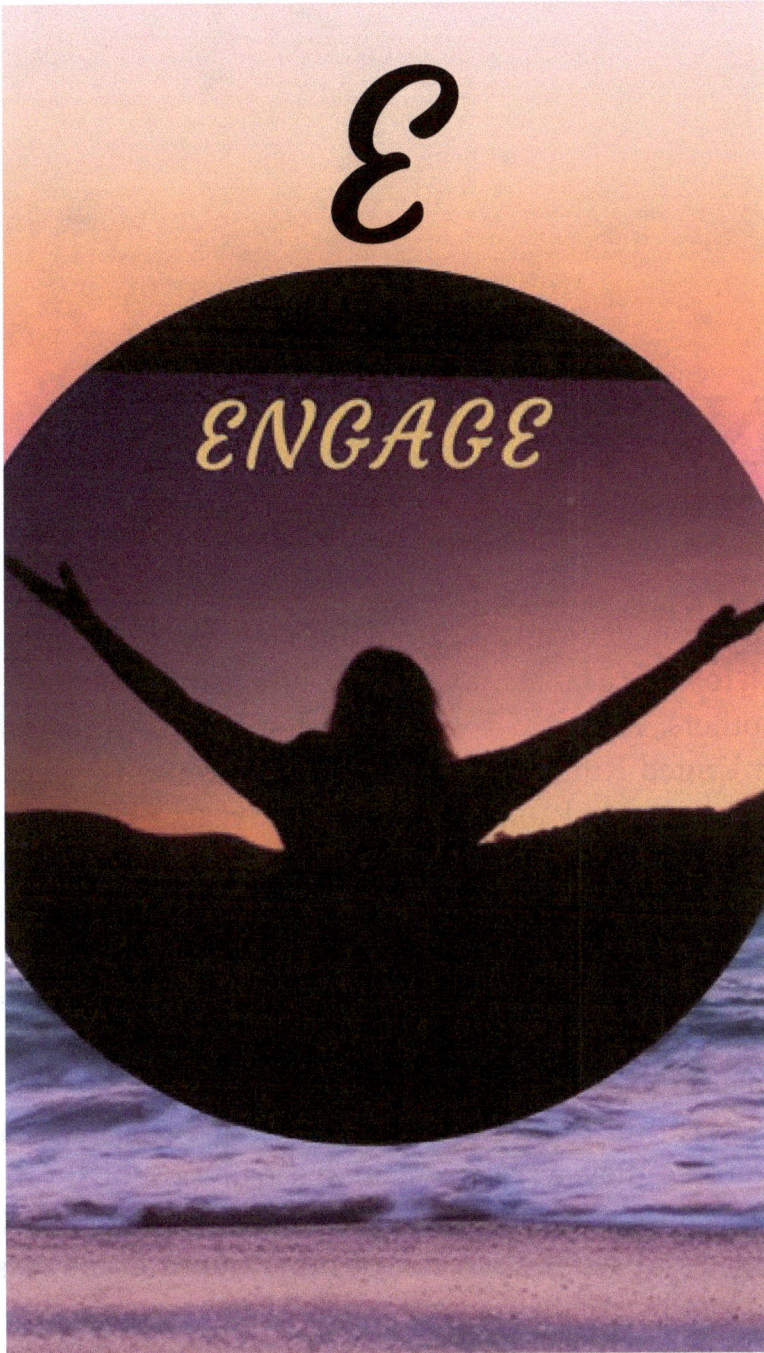

ENGAGE
E is Engage.

Occupy, attract, or involve someone's interest or attention.
Which to me is a fantastic word, because to me it means engage
with others. Recently, I was a guest speaker on a zoom call
to the United Kingdom with 50 Change Youth Leaders from
every country and some as young as 7 years old. Wow, what
they have done and are doing and even were doing during
the pandemic was amazing, they truly are our change leaders
of tomorrow and are changing the world. We can learn from
these dynamic youth while many in the world were stressed
about the pandemic, they looked at the needs and came up
with plans to serve where needed.
It was beautiful to see the background of everyone's flags of
the country they were from, it was truly a global fantastic
experience for me and others on that call and for the youth
themselves to see the passion of other youth of all ages and
ethnic groups. Again, magic happens when we come together.
From that experience an idea was presented to me from one of
my members Lauryn Hunter that GSFE should start a Young

Ladies GSFE network and that she would be happy to be the volunteer director. She has years of expertise working with youth, so we decided what a brilliant idea it is. The meetings are held on Zoom once a month for young ladies from anywhere in the world age 13 to starting college. It is not only a learning experience for the young ladies but for our members as well who are on the meeting call. Being speakers and mentors to these youth who are out leaders of tomorrow.

A great exercise for you would be to put your own words to each of the letters in achieve and see what you come up with. I think you will be surprised as there are so many great words to fit those letters, so which ones are the right ones for you? You never know where an idea will come from, perhaps when you write your own words to ACHIEVE it will spark something for you.

When I was asked to speak on this subject for the Corona Chamber and the response was great everyone said, "Robbie that needs to be your next book." Since I had never done a book all alone, I decided to go for it and to publish it on my 86th birthday March 8, 2022, which is also International Women's Day.

I am stepping up, stepping out, having courage, Showing Up and Asking to continue to ACHIEVE.

If you have a need, always remember to ASK as that is a powerful word and stand back and see action happen which will move you to achieve so much faster. So, keep on achieving and making your dreams come true as everything is possible it's up to YOU.

In the next section you will find some tips to make you a better networker as that will enhance your ability to Achieve and some tips on SHOWING UP and ASKING.

A.C.H.I.E.V.E

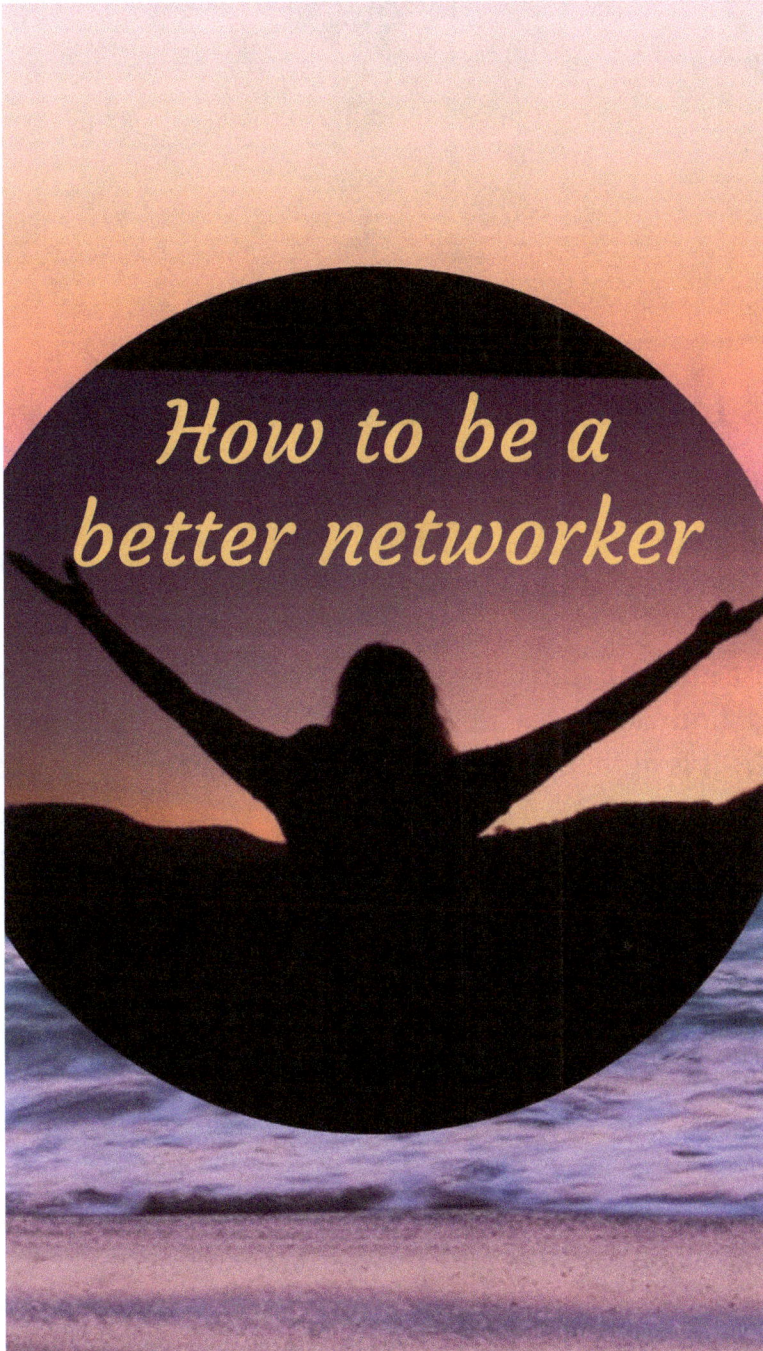

How to be a
better networker

Tips to Help you Network better So you can ACHIEVE Faster

Learning the Art of Networking

Almost all of us must have gotten into a situation when we would find ourselves in a room full of strangers and new people. It is quite an art to socialize instantly with people. But it's not a piece of cake for everyone. So, what can be done? Let us take a look at some tips to help you effectively work a room on your path to ACHIEVE.

Observe And Apply:

Whenever you would be in a situation where all the people in the room in which you are, are strangers to you, begin with observing who is in the room. Who does it look that you would want to meet? Then take action and walk up to that person and tell them you would like to learn about who they are and what they do and how you can support them. The more that you practice this step the easier it gets. Remember it's not about YOU but how you can help them.

Prepare Yourself:

Come prepared with some openers which can be utilized with varieties of people so that you always begin conversing with some new person on an effective note. For e.g. "Which was the last movie that you saw?" and "What was the presentation's most interesting part according to them?" are few good questions for effectively breaking the ice.

Business cards should be kept in plenty, and these should be designed something like mini brochures. Business cards are fabulous conversation starters.

During most of the networking situations, we usually get only a little while for talking about ourselves. A fascinating introduction must be prepared giving brief information about your name, occupation, company name, etc. The introduction must sound natural and not a memorized one.

Stay Confident:

Developing a proper attitude during entering the meeting room is essential for enjoying our outing and creating good marketing opportunities. Begin by noticing how other people enter the gathering. Are they coming in by holding their head high, upbeat and smiling or with eyes down, scared, and serious? By observing this, you can perceive whether they are approachable or not. Compare their body language with yours to know what signals you are sending out to them.

Use The Magic of a Smile and Maintain Eye Contact:

Smiling and maintaining eye contact with someone new to you is essential for breaking the ice. You should always listen attentively to the new person to make him/her feel that you are truly interested. Paraphrasing back and asking questions help in conveying the message that you have understood what they are saying. Smiling and maintaining eye contact are in fact the best non-verbal communication forms for conveying this message. Usually, any type of communication starts with an eye contact as it demonstrates respect. Talking with someone without looking at him/her is difficult as well as disrespectful. Smiling demonstrates a welcoming and non-threatening nature of a person so that a way is paved for either you or someone else for initiating the conversation.

Networking And Not Business Must Be on Your Mind:
You should remember that your prime objective is looking for leads, solving other's problems and exploring new prospects, and not looking for just sales opportunities. Seek people with whom you can network and establish a mutually benefiting marketing relationship. This would require you to talk with just about everyone as you can never tell that what seemed like a dull prospect initially may eventually become the greatest source of your future

Compliment Someone:
Who does not enjoy receiving compliments? You should instantly praise someone or something which he/she possesses if you happen to like it. But you should always be genuine while praising them. As a result, these people will start counting you in their list of good graces and most importantly it will help in initiating a conversation. For e.g., if you happen to admire someone's shoes, then praising them would lead to discussing issues such as their place of purchase and so on ultimately leading to an extensive conversation about shopping and fashion.

Finding Commonality:
All rooms filled with people unknown to each other have one thing in common. All of them are attending the party for the

same reason and many of them would be feeling insecure due to unknown company just as you are feeling. Probably all of them would be friends to the host or maybe working in similar fields. You must identify the commonality and use it for sparking conversations or future relationships. You can identify the commonality between you and someone else by asking questions about their relationship with the host or their job profiles. Conversations start flowing easily after establishing a commonality.

Ask Questions:
Everyone loves talking about himself/herself. Asking questions is a depiction of the fact that you are interested in the talks and issues of others, and it is also a fabulous way of connecting and learning with others. It provides a way for acquiring a particular group or person's "face time." This helps in breaking the discomfort barrier in a big way as the other person also consequently gets interested in your state of affairs. Questions can be simple such as those inquiring about someone's birthplace or first meeting place between them and their spouse. But never get excessively personal with your questions.

It is very important that you should not fake asking questions or even listening. Being genuine is an absolute must in all of your networking approaches and inquiring is no exception.

Offer Assistance:
Helping hands are appreciated by one and all. Offering assistance or help to someone can help you avoid the discomfort feeling arising due to the presence of strangers. Hence, you should always be generous in offering help.

Build Relationships:

The prime objective of networking is building relationships. These relationships can prove to be invaluable in case of future business referrals. Hence, networking must be taken very seriously. For e.g., networking is not all about distributing business cards. In fact, it should never be given unless asked. If you are being asked by someone for your business card, it means that he/she is genuinely interested in you and your business.

Make your presence felt:

Make your presence felt by creating a positive impression of yourself by walking, speaking, or moving around in an elegant manner. You can go for distinctive accessories or interesting clothing styles as per your choice. These are potential conversation starters and people tend to remember you for a long time.

Be articulate:

Be extremely articulate and considerate in whatever you speak about. A precise and concise manner must be chosen for speaking. Rambling and off-the-hook statements must be avoided.

Don't hold on to a single person:

Don't hold on to a single person or few friends for a long-time during networking events. Move around and introduce yourself to more and more people. Sometimes it might happen that you may need to break away from someone who has been clinging on to you for a long time due to your easy-going and friendly nature. During such instances, the clinger can be invited to move around with you. This is a lot easier as compared to simply walking away.

Remember their name:
If the attendees are not wearing badges, you must repeat their name whenever they meet you after the first meeting during the gathering so that you can remember their name.

Follow-up:
You should always follow-up on your help or assistance offers that you have promised someone such as providing a contact or resource. You can send e-mail to contacts that are highly valued providing information about the resource or your observation of some key point during the conversation. This will maintain your existence in their memory. Follow-up plan must be maintained for all the key contacts. Other ways of following up are forwarding links of interesting websites, articles, programs, etc. Asking questions and attentive listening always helps in finding out these interest areas. This helps in maintaining a warm network. Newspaper clippings or magazines having a personal message should never be overlooked. Due to its unusualness these days, it really makes a good impression.

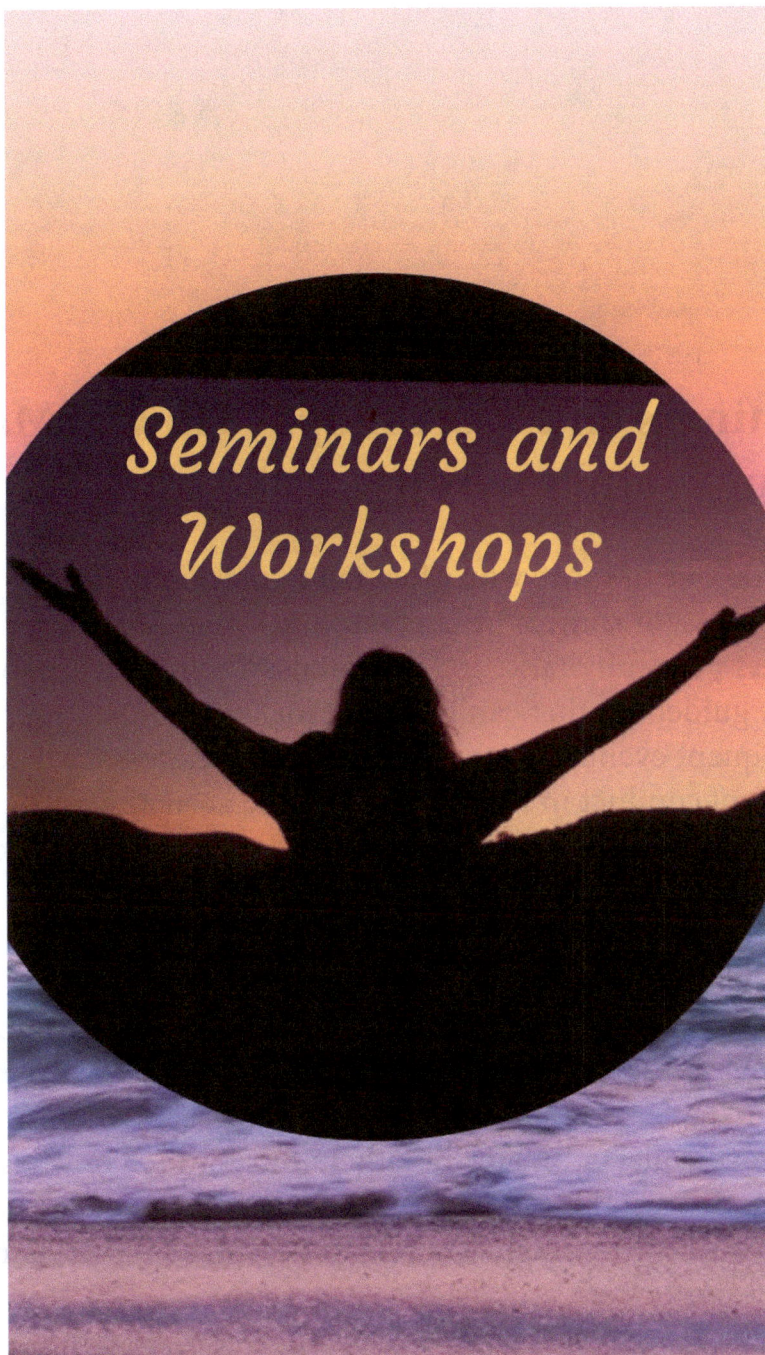

Seminars and Workshops

Seminars and Workshops - How to Make them Useful for You

Are you one of those who often fail to make seminars, workshops, or some other networking events as the events to express your full marketing potentials? Then, here are some of the guidelines that can be useful for you to make your subsequent event money making one. It is necessary to keep a code of conduct in mind while you are at such workshops, business gatherings and conferences. This helps you make the most of attending such an event.

Take Notes for Each Conversation:
It is important for you to know that each conversation or meeting is very important for you, so be careful. After returning to your table, you should take a note of each business card you have collected from the others during the conversation. These notes can be very useful for you soon. These notes may help you link the conversation to the person who is really important to you.

Business Cards Organization:
Make sure, whenever you get some time, you should organize the business cards. You can organize your business cards in different categories like
1. Referrals
2. Potential Customers
3. General
4. Vendors
5. No Use

After categorizing those, when you reach the home, follow up with the person who lies on the first two categories as quickly as possible. You can contact the person who lies in 3 and 4 categories later within few weeks.

Try To Make New Bonds:
During the seminar, you can spend some time with your old colleagues or the coworkers if you must do so. But use the seminars or events for your own good also. Try to be in contact with new people. Try to make some new bonds.

Remember A Person's Name:
It is true that remembering a person's name is a very easy task compared to remembering a ten-digit telephone number or even some lines. We often face difficulties in memorizing some lines or things well, but remembering a name is not a huge task.
Still, we often find ourselves in trouble because of not memorizing the name of a person correctly. May be, at that time we are not fully focused or intended to hear the name of the person. It can often happen that you walk into one room and may be introduced to someone before you get used to the place. It also may be possible that more than one person is

talking to you during your introduction.

Often people get distracted by worrying about some other things like how am I looking? or am I dressed correctly? Those kinds of thoughts can distract any person and that is why they do not hear or memorize the name of several people correctly. Even a handshake can be a big factor for distracting someone. And most of the time, it becomes the main factor of the distraction because a handshake can be too hard, too soft, or too wet and sometimes it can be too cold.

You cannot do much about these kinds of distractions and they are not really in our control; but one thing that is in our control is the ability to adjust. You can always try to make a "Perfect Handshake" that can help you to focus on remembering a person's name.

Few tips and some practice can make you better at memorizing the names correctly. And not only in memorizing the words, but here are also some tips that can be useful to you for improvement in your listening skills and in other areas of the life. You first must understand the difference between listening and hearing.

Listening is Different than Hearing:

Just hearing the name of a person is not enough to remember the name. However, listening can make a difference. One common question comes in every one's mind "What is the difference between hearing and listening"?

It might sound funny, but you can easily find the difference between the hearing and the listening during your routine shower. It is true that you constantly hear the water coming out of the nozzle and cascading into the tub or tile. Pay attention to how water sounds as it falls around you while you wash. Try to identify such nine to ten different sounds. This simple exercise can teach you how to recognize nuances. You now can say that you are listening!

You can find different ways of practicing. One more good practice can be this; while you are listening to a song with fresh ear, don't try to concentrate on hearing the lyrics. Instead of that, try to listen to the musical arrangement. Try to differentiate the instruments used in the music and then try to listen to one instrument at a time. You would be able to eliminate the needless distractions if you find out the right way to listen.

The Use of Mnemonics:

The simplest way to remember the name is to use a mnemonic system. A mnemonic is a memory aid; it uses the relations such as alliteration or a sequence. There are so many types of mnemonics systems such as arbitrary, first letter, visual and assembly.

Visual Mnemonics:

Visual Mnemonics includes the visual triggers or cues. Say for example, if smith is wearing yellow, you might remember him as a yellow smith. This visual effect can fail you. if smith is wearing brown the next time you see him. In simple words, it would be helpful for you to remember the thing related to the visualization.

First Letter Mnemonics:

It also is one simple method to remembering the names correctly. You may remember the name of the person by remembering the initial letters of his name. Say for an example, if you want to remember the name Albert Anderson, you can remember the name by just remembering the initial letters like AA.

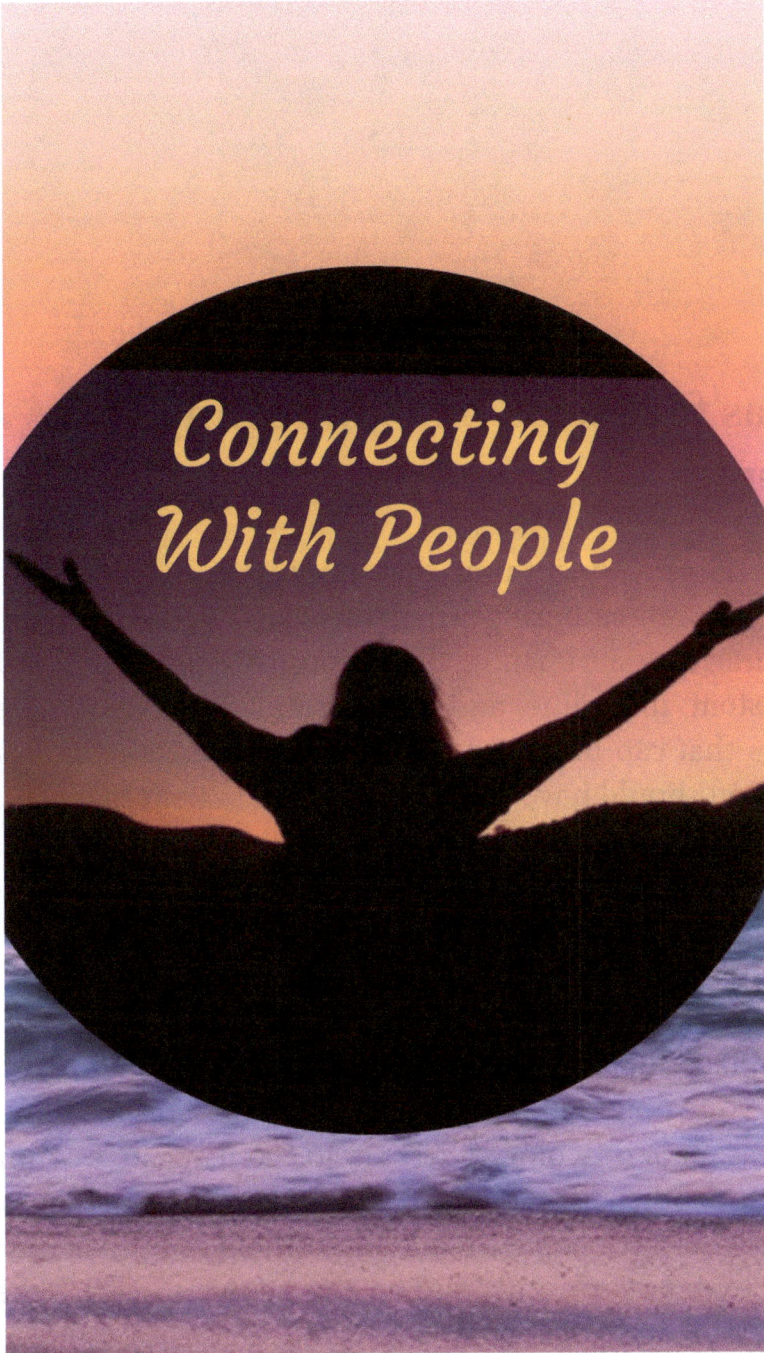

Connecting
With People

Ideas for Focus on Connecting with People

There is only one thing that impresses the people more, than just remembering a person's name. And that thing is remembering a bunch of the names. A desire for the detail, consistent discipline and conversational dexterity are the things that can be useful for making the social contacts. For that, you should have some networking system that can allow you to just focus on connecting with people. Here are some good ideas for networking.

Networking is about them, not you:
Try to make a conversation that is based on the other person. And plan different topics for the conversation in advance. Keep your points upbeat and positive. Do not talk about the unpleasant or off-color topics. Try to avoid negative comments about the other people. Always ask the open-ended questions that encourage people to talk about them and their interests. Whenever you are introducing the people to each other, be thoughtful and generous.

Have several elevator speeches on hand:
Many of you would know about the elevator speeches, but those who do not know about it, here is a small introduction. While you are doing the interactions, the speech comprising the first 15 words is known as an "elevator speech".

You can choose the speech at the right time because it can be related to your job. Another version can be related to your family background. It is up to you to decide which one you need, depending upon the question that has been asked of you. You must choose an appropriate elevator speech that can make a strong impression on the person. Whenever you talk about yourself, be original, upbeat, and brief.

Follow it up with an "urge to action":
Collect the business cards and all the literatures from every person you meet. You can write a quick and useful note to remind yourself about the person, whenever you get sometime alone. You can also note the nick name of the person and what you discussed about; that can help you to follow up with them within some days.

The person would be very impressed, if people find that you have noted detailed information about them, when they get your follow up communication.

Conclusion
You can impress people using your memory. It can also help you to feel good about yourself. You can try doing so and can find how people are amazed if you meet them after some days and are able to remember their names.

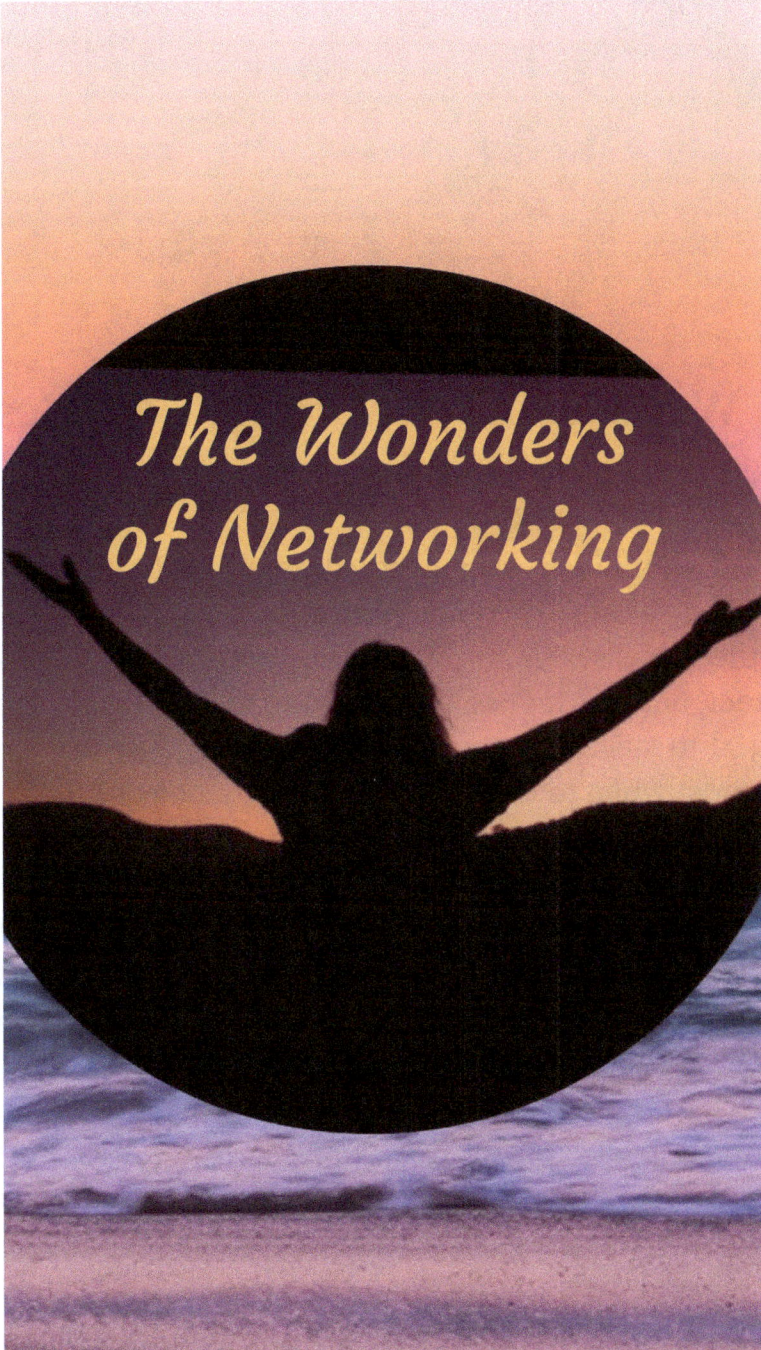

The Wonders of Networking

The Wonders of Networking - The Best Way to Reach Out

Conversing ability really makes a difference. Have you got that knack of speaking to people? Well, it's really an art to speak and put others at ease, and only few people possess it. In business or career, networking is a part and parcel of everyday life. It is essential to sustain work and its flow. Moreover, networking helps most when to think of expanding the business.

Everyone aims to be an excellent communicator for betterment of his or her business and personal life. But networking is not as easy as it sounds. Only select few know how to utilize vocabulary power for effective networks, with the right kind of people. Now don't think only gift of gab is required for a power package. If you think you can get those lucrative contacts by the sole strength of your conversing ability, think again. For a complete package, you need to look very presentable and smart. A handsomely dressed person can attract too many people. The dressing style includes your hairstyle, body language and even the shoes that you wear. You should take care of all little details of personal grooming that may pave way for a successful mark on the people in large and small gatherings, parties, business meets and other seminars, where it becomes important to create a distinct image.

Networking has no limitations; even cultural and social events are essential part of human life. You could make a definite difference in other people's life through your networking abilities and also be volunteering and helping others. And who knows you may find many individuals having similar tastes and likings that you have. Therefore, never do the mistake of limiting your networking to business matters. You may as well mix work, pleasure, and social causes for a wonderful and fulfilling effect.

Networking Is an Art

As can be seen, networking is quite an art. Working your way through a room full of strangers and blending with clusters of people and socializing with them is no stroll in the garden. You have to possess some specific characteristics to become a part of all the action that's going on. Considerable finesse is required for making the changeover from an unfamiliar person to a familiar one.

Key to networking success: Building relationships is the key to achieving success. Our chances of attaining success in any task increases if we are favorable acquainted with a greater number of people. The act of building relationships and making contacts can be made even more effective by joining different business forums and attending their respective networking events. Building relationships and making contacts with people capable of helping you in business or career are the main networking objectives. This is done by listening attentively to answers, asking questions and being aware of problems to be solved sometime later.

Being a great communicator:

You must have the ability to bond people in a pleasant conversation and try to converse with lots of people. Some may find you to be a big bore, whereas some may get hooked to your talking style, therefore moving around in a crowd, and knowing every one of them is a tough job. It is a skill to be able to gel in a gathering, talk to as many people in shortest available time. But give your best smile to one and all; move from person to person without offending them. Remember your time is precious; it should be divided fairly between all the people present there. Do not linger more than necessary near one person just because you feel they are more interesting, even other guests are entitled to your presence. It takes time to perfect the art; but with lots of practice, you may learn to mingle and network better than you did a year back.

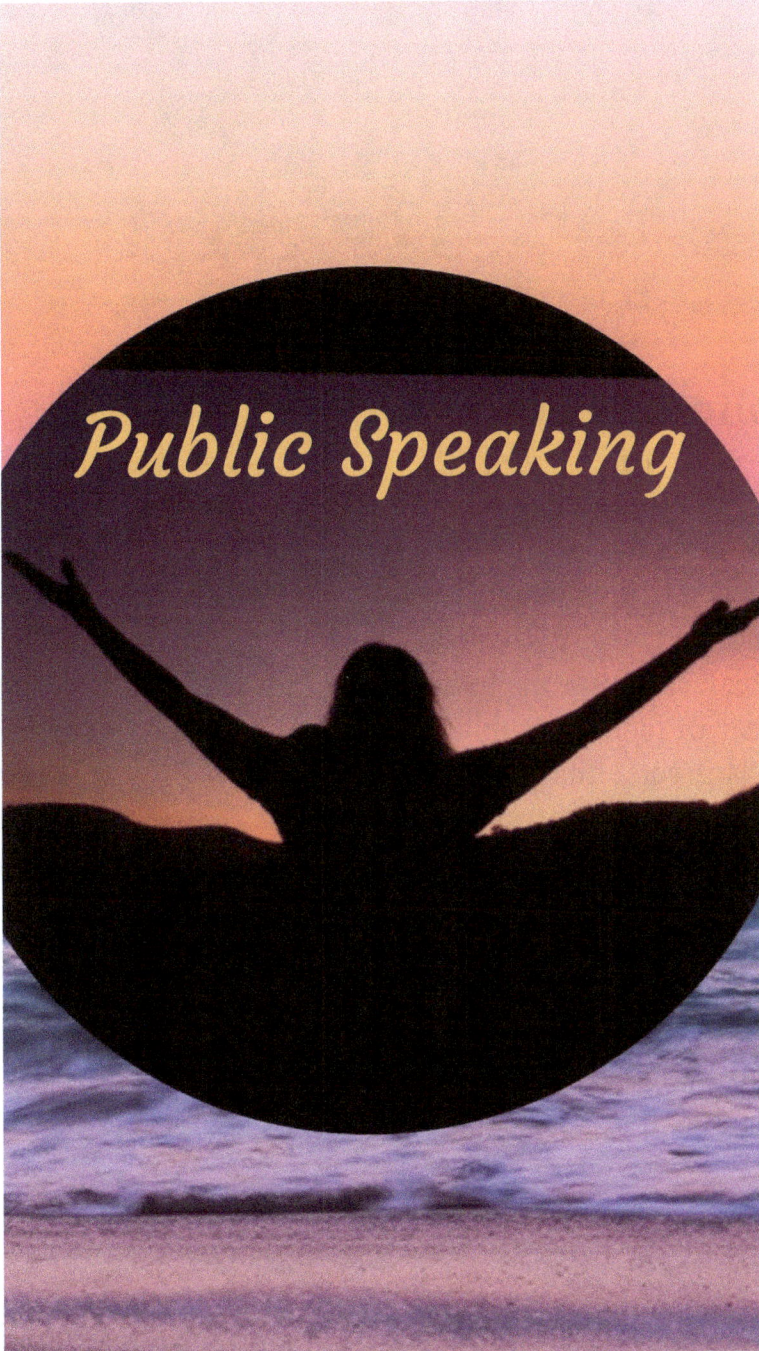

Public Speaking

Public Speaking

We also come across people who are not so comfortable in public. Are you shy of meeting people? Do you fear crowds or feel jittery while facing a large number of people? Well, don't feel isolated, there are many individuals around the world who fear standing up in a crowd and voicing their opinion. The fear of facing a public gathering and speaking in front of them is greater than the fear of disease or even death. Many influential popular speakers are a mass of nerves and anxiety just before their public speech. But when such fear is stretched too long, it becomes a hindrance. Several times, a great speech can be ruined completely due to poor performance or speech delivery. To give that awesome performance on stage, you need a mind-blowing content as well as great oratory skill.

Go through the below-mentioned tips if you really wish to improve your oratory skills:

Deep Resonating Voice:

Practice in a deep voice quality like those of news personalities. An intense and powerful voice carries a lot of weight and authority. If you try and control your breathing, it may lead to a deeper voice. A resonating voice helps in making a good impact and in giving confidence in what you speak.

Speak slowly and clearly: Normally we try to speak in a fast pace when we are anxious and jittery. You may sound nervous and indistinct to the audience. Practice a lot and find a pace that matches your style and comfort level. Speak in a slow and relaxed manner, but not too leisurely that people may feel bored or sleep off. It is always better to have a decently steady pace. Being too fast or too slowly makes the speech incomprehensive and boring.

Bring Variety in Your Voice:

A monotonous dull voice does not interest the audience. You have to bring variations in your voice. Just like when you are singing a song, you pitch it high and low, likewise even during an oration you have to speak with versatility. This will ensure you that the listeners are glued to their seats, mesmerized by the power of your voice. Moreover, voice modulation is important to remove monotony from the speech.

Clarity in Voice:

Public speaking is an art, which you can learn easily. During an oratory session, the voice should be crystal clear and so should be the word pronunciation. A slang tone or an exaggerated accent may spoil your performance.

Adjust Your Voice: I

t is necessary to match your voice volume according to the atmosphere. A high-pitching and loud voice will be akin to shouting, while speaking to a small audience of hardly 10 to 15 members, whereas a soft and low volume will be unheard in a large group of audience with 100 or more listeners.

Correct Pronunciation:

Spell each word clearly with the right pronunciation. If your pronunciation is not correct, the audience may be disappointed with your onstage performance.

Make Contact:

Make correct eye contact with everyone in the audience. Let your eyes roam around rather than be fixed at a single person. Some speakers just refuse to look at the people sitting in front of them, they tend to stare at the wall or their speech notes, which is very irritating and odd behavior.

Gesticulate:

Don't stand like a statue and give your speech. Along with your words, your body should also be able to communicate with the audience. Let your arms and eyes convey what you are talking about. Let your face break into a smile when there is a hint of humor in your speech. The audience will appreciate your efforts and listen to you with rapt attention.

Avoid Lectern :

As far as possible avoid the lectern, which is a hindrance between the audience and yourself. It is best suited, if you do not need any props and it is all between you and the audience. Just try these techniques and you will experience a definite change in your speech presentation. Through continuous practice you may become an excellent orator.

Follow some golden rules to effective networking and communication such as:

Relaxed Approach:

Do not hurry up a conversation with your potential client or business associate; this kind of approach will put them instinctively on guard. They may feel you are pushing your own way into their domain. And no one likes to be bulldozed into doing something by force. So just relax and let the other person also feel the same. If the person is already in deep conversation with someone else, do not try to edge your way into making a threesome. Let him or her complete his talk with the other individual. Once you have the undivided interest of your partner, slowly unwind a casual conversation into a more serious mode that may suit both of your interests. Otherwise, you be tagged as a desperate sort of a person who bombards his/her way for personal gains. This kind of approach gives a wrong negative signal, and you may end up with nothing.

Be Ready:
Many times, we may be caught off guard at parties, social gatherings, or networking events. The most asked question might put you in an embarrassing position like your professional career and prospects. The only way to worm out of it is to be prepared for such queries and if you are really hunting for better job prospects you may very well say so but be sure to coat it with loads of dressings so that you may not be mistaken for a jobless, unsuccessful person. You can always say that you are an adventurous spirit, awaiting a challenging venture to come your way.

Be Tactful:
While exchanging pleasantries at a network event, you may meet many business heads or secretaries who may prove to be very useful in giving potential leads for your professional growth. Do not let such opportunity slip by; use tact and make subtle conversation with such persons and ask in a polite and composed manner, whether they can suggest you to any business prospect or vice-versa. If the answer is in positive,

then feel free to exchange your business card or contact address and ask them their cell number for follow-ups. After this set-up, do not pester them again and again with the same topic, discuss something else, which may be interesting or witty, to make them feel at ease with you. This natural and calm networking may leave a positive impression about you in their minds. And do not spark up a lengthy debatable conversation or bore the other person with some long tale, they may squirm away from you as fast as they can. For good networking chat, the speech should be short but effective.

Be Positive:
You may land up at some networking event where there are hundreds of people you know as well as potential new clients. Instead of trying to escape from the crowd, become more energetic and positive. Talk to as many people you can in the short span of time and try to visualize the new opportunities that have come your way. Say 'oh yes,' rather than 'oh no.'

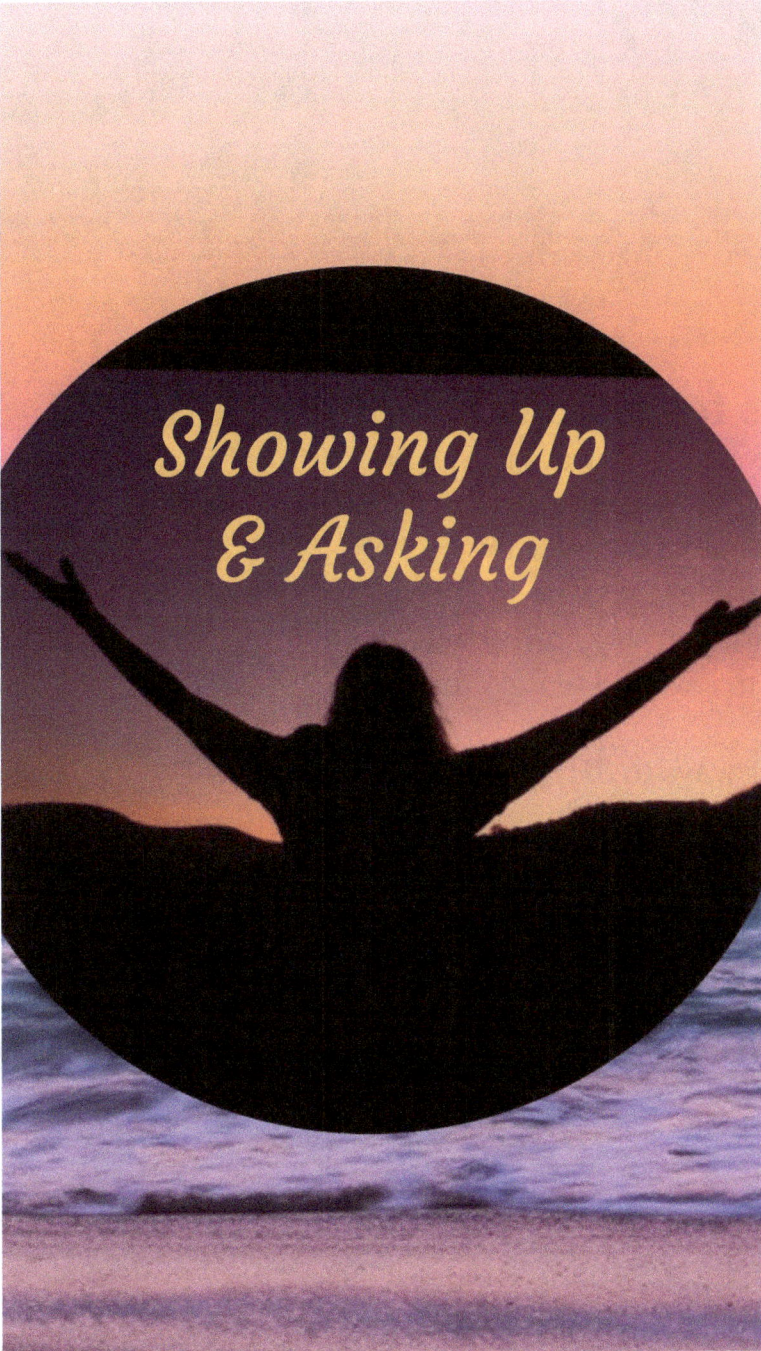

Showing Up
& Asking

Tips for SHOWING UP & ASKING

There are many ways to SHOW UP

First congratulate yourself as you SHOWED UP to read this book and I guarantee by SHOWING UP many exciting things will happen because to me SHOWING UP is like a treasure map, you never know what treasure you will find. I always find treasures when I SHOW UP.

Other ways to SHOW UP

- Attend networking events consistently and follow up with people you meet.
- Be a guest on podcasts, radio, and television shows, as many people today have these opportunities and are always looking for guests.
- Here is an opportunity for YOU to be a guest on a variety of radio shows and podcasts. If you have a show, it is also a great way to get amazing guests. Check out the link https" //www/radioguests.com
- Write a blog post daily, weekly, twice a month, or monthly can be another way to keep you in front of people.
- Speak for groups, organizations, nonprofits, and corporations. Perhaps this could be a start Freespeakersbureau.com

- Write your book or be in a chapter in a book, remember everyone has a book in them, so stop making excuses. If you cannot write you can dictate your book or have someone transcribe the book. That is exactly what one of my members Angeline Benjamin did and she published a beautiful book. She wrote it in a few months.
- Angela Covany, the founder/CEO of Havana Book Group can help you get that book done and published she did it for me and she has lots of talent and expertise in all areas, including designing your book cover. Contact her at hbgpublishing@gmail.com
- Post helpful and engaging stories on face book, Instagram, LinkedIn, and other social media locations.
- Go live on face book every week and provide helpful information and even answer questions.
- Select topics you are good to share.
- Show up places your ideal clients hang out.
- Write articles for magazines and trade journals and other individuals blogs.
- How you SHOW UP is not as important as the fact that you SHOWUP.

If you think that you do not have time to SHOWUP as often as you like it maybe time to take a closer look at how you are actually spending your time. You can find that out by tracking your time for two weeks, capture your activities in 15-minute increments for fourteen days and then check out your numbers.

My challenge to you is SHOWUP, be the most YOU can be. Remember SHOWINGUP fully exactly where you are is the fastest way to ACHIEVE and get where you want to go.

Now that you are SHOWING UP you really need to start

ASKING for what you want and need. So how do you begin doing that?

Remember it's natural to need help, and to allow others to give to you. That's how you work on dropping your ego. Also, you let go of control and great expectations the moment you accept the fact that you need help and ask for it.

I can tell you that ASKING was hard for me as I always was the person that helped others but never ASKED for myself. One day one of my members said, "Robbie do you get pleasure of helping others." I replied, "Yes it fills my heart to know I have touched a life.," the person replied, "well why are you being selfish and not let others help you so they can experience the same pleasure." Wow, that was an eye opener for me and since that day I have learned and applied ASKING and it has become so much easier once I started it.

So how to learn to ASK for Help.

Start small, first know what it is you want, Define the problem, be selective and targeted about who you ASK. The more specific you can be on who to ASK, the better. It's better to ask three people who are very connected than fifteen people who are not interested at all. Do not send an email to your entire contact list. The more specific you can be on WHO should be receiving the message, the better. One direct ASK that results in a YES is better than ASKING fifty people who don't respond. Remember it's good for the other person too, as people like helping others.

Be direct, the easiest way is to simply ASK for what you want and need.

Be okay with rejection, remember not everyone can or is ready to help you, and that's okay, just ASK someone else.

Seek new perspectives. Look at this opportunity to expand your horizons. What others will share with you will be completely different from what you had in mind. It might lead to new ideas or what to do or things that will solve a problem you've been struggling with. JUST ASK FOR HELP!

Find a Mentor, if you like the results with the first small steps, and see that it helps you move forward, you might even think of finding a mentor or giving coaching a try,

Overcome the initial fear. There is nothing wrong with ASKING for help, remember you're looking to get out of a situation or achieve a result, and that won't happen if you don't let someone get involved.
What you can gain by ASKING for help.
You gain the ability to move forward.
You gain the opportunity to collaborate.
You gain the opportunity to learn.
I believe all the steps I have shared with you will be instrumental in helping you to ACHIEVE and soar to greater heights than even you imagined.

I know I will never retire. I love touching lives and making a difference and plan to do it until my last breath and who knows I might just be able to continue my work in heaven, maybe even a GSFE in heaven for all my angel friends.

So, remember you are in charge of your achieving your dream and passion, it's up to you to step out, dream big, get rid of naysayers in your life, cause it's really up to you.

Take bigger steps, dream bigger and totally reap the awards that will come your way, each day work towards your goals and dreams as nothing is impossible.

If you ever read "Think and Grow Rich" then you know this famous quote by Napoleon Hill. "Whatever the mind can conceive and believe, it can achieve."

So, take on the day and go for your dreams and have a magnificent achievement day as there are many miracles waiting to happen for you so SHOW UP, ASK and ACHIEVE,

ABOUT THE AUTHOR

Robbie Motter has been empowering women since 1976. She is the Founder/CEO of the Global Society for Female Entrepreneurs since 2017 and prior to that for 29 years as the NAFE regional coordinator and later becoming the Global coordinator, serving women all over the world. She formed GSFE, her nonprofit in 2017. The GSFE organization now has fourteen networks, two of which are digital to appeal to those not quite ready for those dealing with post covid and/ or in different countries or states that will truly benefit from the wisdom shared from dynamic speakers who choose to share knowledge from the "pay it forward" mentality. Her monthly speakers share from the heart. In January 2022, her organization will have three more chapters coming to fruition. Palm springs, California and Internationally the United Kingdom and Canada chapters. She has truly created an ever-growing sisterhood of women who aim to serve the greater good and recognize one another's potentials and strengths. It is no wonder why the expansion continues to grow. Each of her motivational speakers share in the same mentality of which she stands for, "Collaboration not competition." Her personal motto has always been "We are here to help one another achieve success personally and professionally without personal recognition or gain," as that is the mission statement of the organizations she has been associated with and is involved with. Her passion is to empower, inspire, mentor, educate and connect women so they will become successful entrepreneurs and soar to greater heights than even they could ever have imagined. She is truly an amazing woman. Nothing she does is ever about her gain, only about the women she helps. None of the monthly speakers are paid in GSFE, they are there to serve women globally. GSFE currently has an excess of over 350 members in California and other states as well as Internationally.

She is also the author of a #1 US and International bestselling book "It's All about Showing Up and the Power is in The Asking." Published by Havana book group LLC. It contains forty-six phenomenal Coauthors, all members of GSFE. The book is on Amazon, Barnes and Noble, Walmart, Target, Goodreads, and bookstores all over the world. The funds from the book sales go directly back into GSFE. Robbie's nonprofit was built to serve women. She has also been a co-author in twenty-seven other books over the years. She is currently working on her own book about achieving titled: "How to Achieve, Sub-titled: A Feminine leader's manual for life. It is scheduled to be published on her 86 Birthday March 8, 2022, which is also International Women's Day

Over the years of supporting women, she has been presented with over 160 awards globally by numerous presidents, state municipalities and countless organizations, and the list is ever growing. She is humbled and grateful yet does nothing for recognition. She is an expert connector. A true catalyst of change and a mentor for life. Please reach out to her if you need guidance and mentorship, all who have met her will say she will help you, direct you, and help you change your life!

Connect, Contact and Collaborate with Robbie Motter

globalsocietyforfemaleentrepreneurs.org (G.S.F.E)
Robbiemotter.com
Email; rmotter@aol.com
I am on Facebook and LinkedIn as Robbie Motter & Twitter as Networking queen
Connectedwomenofinfluence.com
Divaregistry.com

HAVANA BOOK GROUP LLC
43537 RIDGE PARK DRIVE
TEMECULA, CA. 92590

COPYRIGHT 2021 All rights reserved.
ISBN: 979-8-9862647-0-7

www.GlobalSocietyForFemaleEntrepreneurs.org

Mission: To empower, inspire, educate and connect women so they become successful entrepreneurs and enjoy fulfilling, productive and abundant lives.

Visit our website to learn more about this amazing international organization.